BASKETBALL HALL OF FAMERS

JERRY WEST

Fred Ramen

the rosen publishing group's
rosen
central

2/04
jB
West
R

For Moe, the fan
And for Kathy, at Webster Village Books,
who made this possible

Published in 2002 by The Rosen Publishing Group, Inc.
29 East 21st Street, New York, NY 10010

First Edition

Library of Congress Cataloging-in-Publication Data

Ramen, Fred.
Jerry West / by Fred Ramen.
p. cm. — (Basketball Hall of Famers)
Includes bibliographical references (p.) and index.
Summary: Profiles the life and forty-year legacy of basketball great Jerry West.
ISBN 0-8239-3482-9 (lib. bdg.)
1. West, Jerry, 1938– —Juvenile literature. 2. Basketball players—United States—Biography—Juvenile literature. 3. Los Angeles Lakers (Basketball team)—Juvenile literature. [1. West, Jerry, 1938–2. Basketball players.] I. Title. II. Series.
GV884.W4 R36 2001
796.323'092—dc21

                                        2001003491

Manufactured in the United States of America

contents

F ew players in the history of the National Basketball Hall of Fame have been as focused on the game or had more of a drive to win as Jerry West. Although he was a player who ultimately became one of the game's top five greatest scorers, West is even better remembered for the way in which he led each of his teams to victory. In his long career, only three times did he play for a team with a losing record, and one of those times was in high school. Each of those teams made the playoffs, however.

In a period when both the country and the National Basketball Association (NBA) were undergoing tremendous changes, Jerry West's

Jerry West, whose exploits with the Los Angeles Lakers earned him the nickname Mr. Clutch, ranks among the most successful guards in basketball history.

smooth jump shot was one thing that the Los Angeles Lakers could rely upon. Yet remarkably, West, a man who was an all-star for every year of his professional career, who twice broke playoff scoring records, and who is generally considered one of the three greatest scoring guards in history, was always more concerned with his team's performance than his own. Although his brilliant performances while under pressure earned him the title of Mr. Clutch, his satisfaction came because he had helped the team win, not because he had sunk the winning basket.

And in one of the greatest ironies in team sports, this man, who so relentlessly drove toward victory, who took each loss personally, and whose incredible clutch performances made the Lakers one of the dominant teams of the late 1960s and early 1970s, won only one championship in his fourteen-year career. He was, however, on a team that many consider one of the greatest in the history of the NBA.

Nor did retirement snuff out West's ache for team success. From 1976 to 1979, he was the coach of the Lakers, leading them to the league's best record in his first year. In 1982, he became their general manager, and his shrewd front office work resulted in four Lakers championships, including back-to-back titles in 1987 and 1988. In 2000, after the Lakers won their first title in twelve years, Jerry West retired, once more leaving the game enriched from his dedication and tireless effort.

Mr. Clutch

Jerry Alan West was born on May 28, 1938, in the little town of Cheylan, West Virginia. The community was too small to have its own post office, and the Wests' mail was delivered instead to Cabin Creek, a neighboring town. This fact would be immortalized in one of Jerry West's nicknames, "Zeke from Cabin Creek," probably given to him by the great Lakers broadcaster Chick Hearn as a reminder of his "hillbilly" origins.

Most of the people in that part of West Virginia worked in coal mines, just barely managing to get by. Jerry West's father, Howard, worked for most of his life for an oil company, however, until many of the oil wells in the area

Laker guard Jerry West makes a layup during an NBA game.

ran dry. He then briefly owned a gas station, but, unable to make ends meet, he eventually became an electrician instead.

Jerry was the fifth of six children. He had two brothers and three sisters. Of his two brothers, Charles and David, he was closer to the younger one, David. David's unfortunate death in 1950, while serving as a master sergeant with the U.S. Army in Korea, was a painful blow to young Jerry, who was only twelve years old at the time. His early experience with death made him extremely introspective, a tendency that he carried with him throughout his life.

West was a shy boy who did not make many friends. He preferred to spend much of his time alone, engaging himself in activities such as hunting and fishing. His family was not particularly close either.

However, from early on West showed that he was a very motivated person. Because his family could not afford luxury items, if he wanted something, other than food or clothing, for himself, he had to earn enough money to buy it himself. In his later years, this same trait would serve him well both on and off the basketball court.

West grew up during a time when baseball was still the most popular professional sport in America. However, the most popular sports team in West Virginia was the University of West Virginia's college basketball team. Even as a young boy, he dreamed of one day playing for them.

First Baskets

Surprisingly enough for a person who would one day play professional basketball, West was very short as a child. He was so small, in fact, that he required vitamin injections from his doctor in order to keep him healthy. Because he seemed so frail, the other children would not let him play football with them. To appease his interest in sports, a neighbor put up a basketball court in his backyard, and West spent countless hours on it practicing in any weather and after school until it was too dark to see the basket anymore. He shot continuously from every possible angle. When he couldn't play with the other children,

Jerry would simply return to the basketball court, endlessly shooting.

As he got older, West tried out for several sports teams at his school. Still small for his age, he didn't make the football or track teams. He played a little sandlot baseball but wasn't particularly good at that either. He did manage to make the junior high school basketball team, however.

West's athletic career hardly began with a bang. The majority of his first two years on the team were spent in the bleachers instead of on the hardwood. But his coach, Duke Shaver, left a lasting impression on him by continually stressing the elements of conditioning and defense, lessons he never forgot.

Team Captain

By his freshman year at East Bank High School, however, West not only broke into the lineup but was also elected captain of his team. Although still raw as a player, his talent and dedication to basic skills was beginning to shine through.

Then, a most surprising thing happened: Over the summer of 1953, he grew six inches. On the one hand, the sudden growth made an already shy person even more self-conscious, and sometimes very clumsy. But, on the other hand, becoming an instant six-footer made him a formidable basketball player almost overnight.

As a sophomore in high school, West missed making the starting lineup on the varsity high school team. But his coach, Roy Williams, helped him apply his raw talent by learning the game both inside and out. It was here that he began to learn the real value of defensive play. Williams also taught West another priceless skill: the value of playing as a member of a team. These lessons would help transform an awkward teenager into one of the most highly regarded high school players in the country.

Still, he suffered a major setback. While attempting to block a shot halfway through the season, West broke his ankle. It was the first injury of a career that would be plagued by them.

Jerry West *(front row, holding basketball)* had a level of integrity, which developed during his early days at East Bank High School, that was practically unmatched in professional sports.

Although he was worried that his ankle might not heal well and that the injury could affect his ability to play, West seemed to take the setback lightly. He broke the ankle again several times while practicing before he was finally able to remove his cast. He was very bored without being able to play basketball. He even tried to stay close to the team by serving as its equipment manager.

East Bank had an excellent season, going 16–4 and playing in the state championship tournament. This left West eager to return to the court for his junior year, but when he did, he faced more obstacles than successes.

His Famous Jump Shot

West became a starting forward on the varsity team, averaging more than 24 points per game. He had abandoned the two-handed set shot of his youth and was now developing his signature jump shot that would one day terrorize the NBA. Still a raw player, he was learning the game quickly, finding out how to shake his defender, how to play defensively, and how to get into position for an effective rebound shot. He scored more than 35 points on three separate occasions, one time making 15 out of 19 shots.

The team, however, was just as green as he was and did not have a very good year, finishing up only 11–13. West was learning another valuable lesson: It's hard to feel good about scoring a bunch of points if your team still loses.

He also suffered his first heartbreaking postseason loss that year, in the first game of the regional tournament. After running up a big halftime lead against a team they had beaten by 20 points earlier in the season, West's team fell apart in the second half and ended up losing the game.

The tough times of his junior year motivated him to work even harder as a senior player. He spent the entire summer and early fall playing basketball and practicing whenever he could. His tireless devotion to improving himself would now pay off in what would become an impressive final year.

Suddenly East Bank had one of the best high school basketball teams in the state. West was in a magnificent groove for the entire season, during which he averaged better than 33 points per game, twice scoring 45. His years of practice and preparation, coupled with his great natural talent, made him nearly unstoppable on the court. Even more important, he had great confidence in himself and was beginning to display a talent for performing exceptionally well under late-game pressure.

This was evident in the fourth playoff game, the regional final against Nitro, the team that had eliminated them during the previous year. This time, however, East Bank was overconfident and trailed by 17 points at halftime. But rallying behind West, who alone scored 12 points in the third quarter, they earned a 5-point win that put them just two games from the championship.

This was East Bank's year, and the team and West were not to be denied. In the final game, he scored 39 of his team's 71 points, despite fouling out with more than five minutes left. The game was won by East Bank, 71–56.

The Scouts Came Knocking

West set a West Virginia high school tournament record in scoring and was now one of the most highly regarded athletic prospects in the United States. Several universities had been scouting him all year long; now they began to make their pitches to him, hoping to attract the lanky boy from a coal-mining town to play only for them. Even better from a recruiting point of view was his solid B average, which meant he would probably not have any problem staying eligible to play during each of his eight semesters.

For the moment, though, West just wanted to bask in the glow of being the best player on the best team in the entire state of West Virginia. His hometown held a parade for the team, and he even made a speech. He felt like a king, but his winning reign would be a short one. It would take sixteen years to win another championship.

He had proven that he was one of the best eighteen-year-old basketball players in the country, but he still had to decide which university offer to accept. He was more than excited to launch the next phase of his career.

It was a critical decision. Playing for a nationally recognized university or college team could put a player in the spotlight and greatly increase his chances of eventually breaking into professional basketball. The right coach, too, could give an enthusiastic player the training necessary to make him an NBA contender.

Yet in the end, it was not such a difficult choice. At the top of his game, West chose to make one of his childhood dreams a reality. All of those years spent shooting baskets long into the night were going to pay off, and the countless times he had dreamed of sinking the big shot for his favorite team were now going to come true. West remembered all the evenings that he had listened to the University of West Virginia's basketball team games on the radio as a child. Now he was going to play for them. He would become a Mountaineer.

Mountaineer

West recalls that approximately sixty colleges attempted to recruit him to play for them. Every major school in the South wanted him; he also received offers from schools in the East and on the West Coast.

Then, as now, recruiting talented players was a competitive business, and the rivalry among the different schools was intense. West can remember coming home one day after a game and finding three different coaches sitting on his front porch. Another coach literally broke down in tears, practically begging West to come play for his team. In the end, despite flirting with schools such as Texas A&M and Maryland University, he made the decision to attend the University of West Virginia.

West's constant practicing and personal ideals gave him confidence in his approach to the basket.

Undoubtedly, this was due in large part to the fact that it allowed him to fulfill his dreams of starring for his local team. For the shy, introverted West, it may also have been a comfort to remain in his home state, where he was regarded as a local hero, rather than moving to a strange new place where he would have to struggle to prove himself. Certainly, his mother was pleased that he remained close to the family in West Virginia.

But even at eighteen years of age, West was ambitious and driven. He realized that he was a special athlete with a good chance of making it to the professional league. Having grown up in a family that struggled to have even the most basic necessities, he desired financial success. In order to achieve it, though, he needed to join a team that would bring him national prominence, pitting him against top competitors so that he could prove himself at the highest level. He needed to make the scouts from the NBA pay attention. Whatever his desire to remain in his home state, it seems unlikely that he would have jumped to West Virginia had the university not begun to rise to national prominence.

College Basketball

The college game in the 1950s was very different from the game we see today. Although many of the teams that today continue to dominate the National Collegiate Athletic Association (NCAA) Tournament were powerhouses then—such as the University of Kentucky—it was also a time when smaller colleges, with smaller reputations for delivering strong athletic teams, competed at the highest level. For example, New York University (NYU), which today plays in Division III, won an NCAA title during West's last year in college.

West Virginia's teams had been steadily improving during the 1950s. Led by coach Fred Schaus, a former basketball star at the school, the team had even fielded a few all-American players during a period when being selected was considered one of the highest athletic honors in the United States.

The team's star, Rod "Hot Rod" Hundley, was probably the best player in the school's history. He helped to recruit West, who was flattered that West Virginia's top athlete would take a personal interest in him. Coach Schaus, who was more interested in another player, a big center named Willie Akers, listened to Hundley's advice and offered West a scholarship. (Akers would also join West at the school; they had become friends while playing together in several all-star games over the summer.)

Campus Life

College was a big change for West. For the first time in his life he was on his own, living away from his family. Always shy and withdrawn, he had a hard time adjusting to college life and being separated from his friends. But soon he got caught up in life on campus and plunged himself into basketball.

In those days, freshmen were not allowed to play on the varsity squads, so during his first year, West played on a separate freshman team.

Jerry West, a forward for the University of West Virginia Mountaineers, jumps to block an opponent's shot during an NCAA basketball game.

They went 17–0, and West led the team in scoring with 19 points per game. Surprisingly, West, smaller in size than many college athletes at six feet three inches and 165 pounds, also led the team in rebounding. This was due to his quickness, jumping ability, and fearlessness under the basket. It was also a tribute to his hard work in studying all parts of the game, especially defense, which was West's trademark.

During the off-season, West worked a variety of odd jobs set up by fans of the university. Most of the jobs required him to show up somewhere and do a little work or make public relations appearances, such as playing for company teams. While slightly questionable and probably against NCAA rules, this star treatment must have been an enormous boost to a poor boy from a small town.

The next year, he joined the varsity team and soon became its starting forward. For the first time, he was facing top competition from all parts of the country, and he had to make many adjustments in his game, unlearning bad habits from his younger days, while all the time struggling to learn the fundamentals. He has described this as his most difficult season, although in some respects it was his most successful one.

Honing His Skills

In the 1957–1958 season, Coach Schaus's team was thoroughly balanced. Although Hot Rod Hundley had played his last season (moving on to a career with the then Minneapolis Lakers),

Hot Rod Hundley, who played a key role in recruiting Jerry West to the University of West Virginia, poses for one of many NCAA publicity shots.

Schaus still had six-foot-ten-inch center Lloyd Sharrar and a quick team that included promising young players like West and Willie Akers. The previous year's team had won the first Southern Conference title in the school's history. Not only would they win the title again in the 1957–1958 season, but they would also go undefeated within their own conference and on their home court. (While West was at the university, his team had a forty-three game home-winning streak; he never played in a home game they lost.)

Personally, the year was one of struggle and growth for the young athlete. He averaged almost 18 points per game and improved defensively. He struggled early in the season, but in a game against Richmond, he broke out with 28 points, including a basket that tied the game with only seconds remaining, and then earning an additional 7 points during overtime.

But if West had his struggles, the team did not. Picked by many to be a strong contender, Schaus's squad surprised everybody that year. A key moment came during the Kentucky

Invitational Tournament, held during the winter break. West Virginia beat a favored Kentucky team on their home court and then won the tournament final. This gave them an eight-game winning streak to start the season.

The streak would eventually reach fourteen games, including a miraculous comeback on the road from 14 points down with eight minutes to play against Villanova University. West scored a season-high 37 points, including 17 of West Virginia's last 23, and made the game-winning assist.

At the end of the season, West Virginia was 21–1—the school's best record in history to that date—and became the number-one ranked team in the entire country. It was an impressive introduction to big-time college ball for the sophomore from the little town of Cheylan.

But that year also brought heartbreak for West. The school's magnificent season crashed hard once the squad got to the NCAA Tournament. An unheralded Manhattan team beat them in the first round, 89–84. It was a crushing blow to everybody associated with the team, especially after an entire season of hard work. Even worse, the national champion that year was the same Kentucky team that they had beaten earlier in the season.

Still, there was nothing to do but think of next year. West's junior year of college would be very different. For one thing, he would become the star of his team, making University of West Virginia a notable college contender.

Collegiate All-American

Big Lloyd Sharrar graduated after the 1957–1958 season, and Coach Schaus went with a smaller lineup. But they were also quicker, able to put excellent defensive pressure on other teams and capitalize on the turnovers this created. West was now the definite star of the team and its leader, and he responded with an excellent season.

The team struggled early on. Returning to the Kentucky Invitational Tournament, they

Jerry West unleashes a jump shot against George Washington University during a Southern Conference game in Washington, D.C., on March 1, 1958. His team, the University of West Virginia, would go on to win the title that year.

made it to the final but lost to Kentucky this time. West scored 36 points in the game, though. The team lost again, this time to Northwestern, in one of the worst games of his college career; he scored only 17 points.

In the Mountaineers' next contest, though, West made 17 of 25 shots, and 10 of 11 from the foul line, scoring a career-high 44 points. After, they would lose only one more game, a double-overtime thriller to NYU in Manhattan's famed arena, Madison Square Garden.

West's scoring that year put him in the elite of all college players. He shot more than 50 percent from the field on the way to averaging over 26 points per game. He also led the team in rebounding and threw in almost 100 assists. He made all-American that year and was named both the Southern Conference's player and athlete of the year.

But as was usual for West, the individual awards didn't mean as much to him as the team's overall performance. This year he had much more to be proud of, yet the Mountaineers still fell short of winning it all, a crushing disappointment to the newest all-star.

The Mountaineers cleared the opening rounds easily, marching past Dartmouth in the opening game. In their second romp, a tenacious St. Joseph's squad had them down by 18 points with thirteen minutes left in the game. Desperate enough to try anything, Coach Schaus had West play in the center position; he responded with 14 points in the next four minutes. Later, he would score the go-ahead basket and sink two critical free throws that would seal the victory. Another strong performance against Boston University, where he scored 20 points in the second half, led them into the Final Four.

MVP Sensation

Against the University of Louisville, West had another magnificent game, scoring 38 points and pulling down 15 rebounds despite taking only six shots in the second half, as West Virginia cruised into the final game. For the first time, West would take the national stage with a championship game on the line. And for the first time, the United States would get to see his private heartbreak played out on this most public of stages.

A bad start doomed West Virginia in the final game. The University of California–Berkeley, led by West's future Los Angeles Laker teammate Darrell Imhoff, drove a defensive strategy that was a tough nut to crack for Schaus's wide-open

offense. Yet they made a strong run late in the game. Playing with four fouls, West led a comeback that brought West Virginia within one point. He was lined up for the game-winning basket when time ran out. Once again, this supreme clutch player was denied a chance to pull out one more win.

For his efforts, though, West was named the tournament's most valuable player. He had established himself as not only one of the best college players but a terrific man to have on court when the pressure was on. His senior season at West Virginia promised to be even better.

Now with two years of experience under his belt, West began what was to be his most impressive college season. But even though his numbers were better than ever, it still held a whirlwind of personal problems for the college hero.

For the third straight year, West Virginia played for the championship of the Kentucky Invitational Tournament over the winter break. Avenging the previous year's loss, the team

Darrell Imhoff of the University of California reaches through the hoop to retrieve the ball as Oscar Robertson (number 21) watches.

triumphed 79–70, with West scoring 33 points and pulling down 18 rebounds, despite having his nose broken during the game. It was the first of many times that he would have to play with an injury.

One big moment in this season came in a home game against Villanova University. For the first time in West Virginia's history, an African American man played basketball on their court: Villanova's George Raveling. The friendly handshake and hug West gave Raveling probably helped relieve what could have been a tense situation for both sides.

Although the Mountaineers had a fine season, finishing up at 21–4, they were more inconsistent than during previous years. For the first time in his college career, West's team lost games in their own Southern Conference, losing to both the College of William & Mary and George Washington University. Still, they were ranked at number six nationally and were once again considered a strong contender for the national title.

For the season, West averaged over 29 points and 17 rebounds per game. Once more he was an all-American, as well as the Southern Conference's player and athlete of the year. Everything was going his way, but disappointment lurked in the postseason.

West Virginia won its first game easily, beating Navy 94–86. They only had to beat NYU to advance to the final game for the second straight year. Earlier in the year, they had trounced NYU 98–69 at home. But this game would prove to be much tougher.

The Battle for the Win

The game was an epic struggle. Late in the match, West Virginia led by two. NYU's Russ Cunningham tried to shoot over West, who blocked the shot. But it came right back to Cunningham, who sank a game-tying shot that took the game into overtime.

In the final seconds of overtime, the lead seesawed back and forth. West went in for a layup shot that put West Virginia ahead by two points. NYU came back with a steal that led to two unanswered buckets and then added a foul

shot for a three-point lead. West passed the ball to a teammate who scored to cut the lead to one. West Virginia managed to get the ball back with just a few seconds left. West took a pass and sent up a jump shot that hit the rim and bounced out just as game time expired. One of the game's best clutch shooters had missed when it counted most.

It helped very little that they won the consolation game—a contest between the losers of the semifinal games—the next night, or that they at least had lost to the eventual champions. Once more West would have to walk away from a season without a championship.

But there was much more to which he could look forward. As one of the top three players in college basketball, he was a certain NBA draft pick. And as a further honor, he had been invited to play for the U.S. national team that would compete in the 1960 Olympic Games. The next few months would introduce many exciting and interesting challenges to him, and once again he would have to prove his game at a new level—and a new position.

University of West Virginia forward Jerry West prepares to make a pass during a college basketball game.

3

Rookie

There was little doubt that West would be an early selection in the upcoming NBA draft. But before his professional career even started, two life-changing events happened to him: He played in the 1960 Olympics in Rome, Italy, and he got married.

The Olympics

He already had some experience with international competition. After the 1959 college season, he had played in the Pan-American Games, helping a United States team beat Brazil for the gold medal in a very close game. But the Olympics were obviously a more prestigious event, giving him the chance to shine on the worldwide stage. And the 1960 U.S. Olympic basketball team was one of the greatest in the history of the Games.

In those days, the rules strictly prohibited professionals from playing in the Olympics. The basketball team was mostly made up of top college players, as well as men from the armed services and the better amateur leagues that still existed in the country. West was one of seven college players named to the squad.

Many people consider this team to be the greatest U.S. Olympic basketball amateur team ever. (Professional players were not allowed to compete until 1992.) Ten of its twelve members went on to play in the NBA, and three of those— West, Oscar Robertson, and West Lucas—would eventually enter the Basketball Hall of Fame.

The 1960 team was, simply put, far and away superior to the rest of the world's Olympic teams. They won every game by at least 24 points, and the average margin of victory was more than 42 points. They marched easily to the gold medal.

Jerry West *(second from left)* and Oscar Robertson *(second from right)* receive congratulations from competitors from the Soviet Union and Brazil after leading the United States to Olympic gold in 1960.

Playing in Rome and getting to see the greatest athletes in the world was a heady experience for the twenty-two-year-old from a coal-mining town in West Virginia. And he had a chance to get to know many of the people whom he would play with and against during his professional career, especially the man many consider the greatest all-around basketball player of his era: Oscar "the Big O" Robertson, who had played for the University of Cincinnati during his college career. West and the Big O were destined to have many exciting confrontations with each other during a long professional rivalry.

A Hero Returns

Returning to West Virginia, West received a grand welcome. The town of East Bank, where he had played in high school, renamed itself "West Bank" for a day. The governor of the state invited him for a visit. For a long time after the Olympics, people continued to invite West to dinners and receptions.

But more than his Olympic success made him happy in those days, he had also recently wed.

His wife, the former Martha Jane Kane, had also been a student at the University of West Virginia. West remembered liking her the first time he saw her, although he was still so shy that it took a while until he worked up the nerve to ask her for a date through a mutual friend. Until that point, he had had very few dates in high school and college.

Jane (as she liked to be called) and West immediately became friendly. She didn't know that he was a star basketball player for the university, which pleased him. He wanted someone to like him for himself, not because he was a "big man on campus." In fact, West remained a loner for his entire college career. He never joined a fraternity and had few friends. Although the school had a bit of a reputation for having students who liked to be rowdy, West never experienced those wild times. During his last two years in college, he

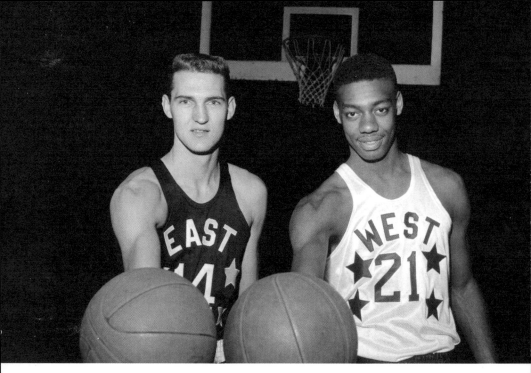

Jerry West enjoyed a special friendship and an exciting rivalry with Oscar Robertson throughout college and his professional career.

lived with two elderly sisters who took in athletes as boarders.

West was, then as now, intensely self-critical and very demanding of himself and of others. He is, he has admitted, not always an easy person to be around. But with Jane he was able to relax and be himself. They would eventually have three sons together.

Getting married is usually a major point in a young man's life. But in West's case, the future was even more exciting and frightening because he was also getting ready to enter the professional level of competition: the NBA.

The NBA, Then and Now

The league West was going to join was different in many respects from the one we are familiar with today. It was much smaller and contained only eight teams. Many of these teams played in different cities than they do today. For example, the Warriors, who now play in Oakland, once played in Philadelphia. The city of Syracuse in upstate New York (which remains a basketball hotbed thanks to its usually strong college team) boasted their own professional franchise, the Nationals, who would eventually take the place of the Warriors in Philadelphia and change their name to the 76ers.

Another team that was on the move was the Lakers, who played at the time in Minneapolis. (In fact, their name is a reference to the state nickname of Minnesota: the Land of 10,000 Lakes.) Early in their history, they had dominated the NBA with teams that included such stars as Jim Pollard, Verne Mikkelson, and George Mikan, the six-foot-ten-inch "giant" who was the league's first great big man. But since those days, the franchise had fallen on hard times and was considered one of the worst teams in the league.

The NBA itself was struggling. It had nearly folded several years earlier, unable to shake its reputation for rowdiness. Playing in arenas so small that chicken wire "cages" were erected along the sides of the court to prevent fans from getting hit by loose balls didn't help that reputation either. Fans often thought that the rowdy players were so aggressive that they deserved to be put in cages, and the circumstances provided an obscure nickname—"cagers"—for basketball players.

Making matters worse, fan attendance was at a critical low. Players would often avoid direct contact and therefore not take high-risk shots. They would simply give the ball to their best ball-handlers, who could dribble it for long periods. The only way to get the ball back was to foul the dribbler; after his free throws, the other team would start doing the same thing, dribbling the ball and playing "keep-away" until they were fouled. Very few points were scored, and nobody felt excited about the games. Luckily, the invention of a shot clock, which forced each team to at least try and make a basket within twenty-four seconds or give up possession (an innovation that took place in the 1954–1955 season), improved the game's pace and started to make it popular again.

The Golden Age

The style of play in the league West was about to enter was also somewhat different from today's game. It was more freewheeling, with far less emphasis on defensive play. Most teams played man-to-man defense, rarely double-teaming; it was a point of honor for each player to be able to cover his own man.

Although many fine athletes played during this time—which, in many respects, was a golden age for the NBA—the overall talent level was probably not as high as it is today. This was rapidly changing as a more diverse group of talented athletes was beginning to represent the league. However, the era was dominated by only a few players who were each able to accomplish some unbelievable feats: the Milwaukee Bucks' Wilt Chamberlain, for example, scored 100 points all by himself in a game against the New York Knicks during a season in which he averaged 50 points per game. That same year, Oscar Robertson averaged a triple-double (ten or more rebounds, points, and assists) per game. In a Finals game against West's Los Angeles Lakers, Bill Russell pulled down 40 rebounds.

The team to beat throughout this period was the Boston Celtics, led by future Hall-of-Famers like Bob Cousy, Sam Jones, K.C. Jones, John Havlicek, and especially Russell. They would win the championship eleven times in thirteen years.

Then, as now, the league assigned draft choices based on how poorly a team did in the regular season. The top three players in college in 1959 were Oscar Robertson, a forward for the University of Cincinnati; Jerry West, who at that time was also a forward; and Darrell Imhoff, who played in the center position for the University of California. The first three picks in the draft belonged to the Cincinnati Royals (now the Sacramento Kings), the Minneapolis Lakers (who were about to move to Los Angeles), and the New York Knicks, in that order. Robertson was guaranteed to go to Cincinnati. But West thought that the Lakers would take Imhoff, since they needed a center, which would allow him to go to New York.

New York City intrigued West because it was, just as today, the center of the national media. He had played there several times during his college career and respected the fans who were so knowledgeable and passionate about basketball. The Knicks were not a particularly good team and had no huge

Bob Cousy of the Boston Celtics
hops for a layup against the New
York Knicks during an NBA
game on November 25, 1961.
Cousy and the Celtics dominated
Jerry West and the Los Angeles
Lakers throughout the 1960s.

stars, so he would have a chance to really shine. For someone who always hungered to make a name for himself, the advantages of playing on such a huge stage were tempting.

That said, he was somewhat disappointed when the Lakers selected him instead of Imhoff with the second pick of the draft. In the end, however, it was one of the best things that could have happened, not only for his career but for the entire league.

Although the Lakers had a weak record the year before, there were reasons to hope that they could improve. One of those reasons was their magnificent small forward, Elgin Baylor, a creative player and among the first to bring an acrobatic component to the game. Baylor was a scoring machine who would become part of a formidable tandem with West—the "Mr. Inside" to West's "Mr. Outside."

Part of West's disappointment with being drafted by the Lakers was that they were still in Minneapolis at the time. It was not until he was in Rome for the Olympics that he found out that they were being moved to Los Angeles. This made his prospects much more exciting— Los Angeles was a media center second only to New York City. If he couldn't play on Broadway with the Knicks, then he could try Hollywood with the Lakers. True, Los Angeles was not known as a basketball town, and it would be a challenge to generate interest among its fans, but West was hardly a person to back away from a challenge.

His Rookie Season

Two other factors would help ease him into his first few years in the NBA. One was the presence of Hot Rod Hundley, the former West Virginia star who had helped recruit him for coach Fred Schaus of the West Virginia Mountaineers. The other was Schaus himself, who had just been hired to coach the Lakers. Having Schaus as his coach probably also helped West make the transition from the forward position, where he had played during high school and college, to his professional position as a guard.

At first, the change was a difficult one. At six feet three inches and 170 pounds, West was simply not tall enough to play forward in the NBA. Furthermore, his innate quickness would actually be a greater asset in the guard position. His greatest problem was ball handling; this had always been the weakest part of his game, but he worked at it constantly and remained a consummate team player.

In time, West came to prefer his new position because it allowed him to play facing the basket throughout the entire game. Furthermore, it put him right into the flow of the competition, since he was often responsible for bringing the ball upcourt, leading the fast break that became a Laker trademark. In those days, the roles of the two guards had not become as rigidly separated as they are today; West became the leader of his team's offense and led it much as modern point guards do today. Later in his career, both he and Lakers guard Gail Goodrich would average more than 20 points per game, statistics that would put them in the top 5 percent of the league. Indeed, when asked today whether he thought of himself as a point guard or a shooting guard, West invariably responds, "I played guard." (For the record, the great point guard of the Knicks, Walt "Clyde" Frazier, thinks that both West and Robinson were closer to modern shooting guards than point guards.)

Still, the transition to the professional game was a very difficult one for West, far worse than any other season he had ever had. He did not begin the year as a regular, which hurt his pride, especially since he demonstrated that he was better than the team's other players once he was allowed to compete. The high level of competition in the NBA also required a great deal of adjustment. Every night he faced players who had been stars on their own college teams and were now merely ordinary professional athletes. To top things off, he had to face players who were the absolute best in the

Frazier (with a little help from his teammate Wilt Chamberlain) on his way to making a basket in an NBA playoff game in Los Angeles on April 26, 1972.

world. The rough-and-tumble physical nature of the NBA also took some adjustment.

Even though the early going was difficult, West made the All-Star Game during his rookie year, which was an honor. (It was just the beginning for him, though: He made the team every one of his fourteen years in the NBA.)

His reputation as a clutch shooter was also growing. In one game against Cincinnati, he lost the individual scoring duel with his opposing guard, Robinson, but drove around the future Hall of Famer in the final seconds to sink a game-winning shot.

The Playoffs

Although the Lakers finished with a losing record, they still made the playoffs. They beat the Detroit Pistons in the first round and moved on to face the St. Louis Hawks. The Hawks, led by Bob Pettit and Clyde Lovellette, were a big, strong, physically intense team. But the much smaller Lakers upset the Hawks in the first game. Although the Hawks came back twice to tie the series, the Lakers were still ahead by three games to two when Game 6 was played in Los Angeles. Unfortunately, they lost a heartbreaker by one point in overtime, 114–113. Game 7 was nearly as close, with neither team able to break out in front, but when Elgin Baylor missed what would have been the game-tying shot in the final seconds, the Lakers were doomed.

West's rookie season was over. He ended up second on the team in scoring, though with only 17 points per game. In the playoffs, however, he had averaged over 23 points a game, a sign of things to come. More important, the team had surprised everyone, taking a superior St. Louis squad to the brink of elimination. There were many good signs in the air. Next year's Laker team would be the one to watch.

They would indeed, and much of the fanfare was generated by West. He and the Lakers were about to embark on a quest that would last nearly twelve years and include

Soon after joining the
NBA, West gained the
respect of his competitors
for his dogged
determination to score
and win.

nine appearances in the NBA Finals, start one of the greatest rivalries in the history of professional sports, and build a fervent basketball following in an area where it hadn't before existed. Yet in the midst of all this success would be recurring failure at the very end, a frustrating and maddening course of events for West and an entire city.

Champion

Just as he had at University of West Virginia, West would improve his game substantially during his second year in the pros. And the Lakers would also do much better, blowing open their division and winning it hands down. It was quite a turnaround from the year before.

They did it despite losing Elgin Baylor at midseason when he was called up to join the army. In his six-month absence, West took the leadership of the club, filling the huge scoring hole. During a game in January 1962, he scored 63 points, which, at the time, was a record for a guard.

In the playoffs, the Lakers easily pushed the Detroit Pistons aside to go to their first NBA Finals in Los Angeles. They would face the Boston

Celtics, who were going for their fourth consecutive NBA title.

The Boston Celtics

The legend of the most famous basketball team of all, the Boston Celtics of the 1960s, remains undimmed, even after nearly forty years. Their title run was one of the greatest in the history of professional sports, possibly even more impressive than the Yankees twice winning five consecutive World Series. As in the Yankees' success of the 1950s, the Celtics were a team of skilled players built around one all-time great, Bill Russell, who is still considered the best defensive center to ever play basketball.

Beating the Celtics would be a tall order for any team, especially the upstart Lakers, with their wide-open playing style. Remove Baylor and West from the game and the Lakers would have no answers. In contrast, the Celtics had no single high-scoring player. At the end of the game, however, opponents would look up at the scoreboard and see that five or six Celtics had scored in double figures. They had so few weaknesses and so many strengths, especially their deep and versatile bench. How many teams could play a future Hall of Famer—John Havlicek—as their sixth man?

But in their first confrontation, Los Angeles and Boston played an epic series that would set the tone for all their future battles.

Grace Under Pressure

They split the first two games in Boston. In the first game at Los Angeles, the Celtics led by 4 points with one minute left to play. West nailed a jump shot to trim the lead to only 2, and when the Celtics failed to score on their next possession, he calmly sank another basket that tied the game. With three seconds remaining, the Celtics called time out, hoping to set up the winning shot. Instead, West took a gamble, stole the inbound pass, and raced up the court, getting off a hurried shot that went in for the game-winner.

He had scored the last 6 points by himself and made a brilliant defensive play. This was perhaps the moment when the legend of Mr. Clutch was born—a nickname that West never liked.

Once again they split the next two games, and when the series returned to Los Angeles, the Lakers had a chance to close it out. But the Celtics proved too resilient, winning by 14 points to set up a dramatic Game 7 confrontation.

Just as in Game 3, it was a tense contest right to the very end. With only eighteen seconds left, the score was tied. And just as in Game 3, the Celtics lost the ball. But West didn't take the final shot. Instead, Frank "Pops" Selvy, who had scored the Lakers' last 4 points (including the game-tying basket) took a short shot from the left of the basket. If he made it, the Lakers would win. But he missed. The Celtics pulled out a three-point win with a final score of 110–107.

Would things have been different if West had taken that final shot? It was a question that haunted him for the rest of his career. On one hand, he always wanted to have the ball at the end of the game. And he had already shown that he was one of the best players in league history under high-pressure circumstances.

On the other hand, he knew that the Celtics would do anything to keep him from getting the ball in that situation. In such circumstances, the best way he could help the team was to make it possible for his teammates to gain control. Selvy had been hot, and who knows if West would have hit the shot? In a similar spot just two years before, he had missed a game-winning shot against NYU in the final moment.

Mr. Clutch and His Losing Lakers

As crushing as that series was, consider this: Los Angeles played Boston five more times in the next seven years, losing every time. Twice more they would play a seventh and deciding game against Boston. And lose. Toss in another seventh game loss, this time in 1970 to the

Knicks, and you have perhaps more heartbreak than any professional athlete should be asked to bear, certainly not one as sensitive and as fiercely hungry to win as West. He became the only player to ever win the Finals MVP award who played on a losing team.

In the classic 1969 Finals game against Boston, West sunk what should have been the winning shot but wasn't. He always referred to it as "a beautiful thing, wasted."

They called him Mr. Clutch, the greatest clutch shooter in the league, and one of the two or three greatest in the history of the game. (Among modern players, only Michael Jordan and perhaps Earvin "Magic" Johnson or Larry Bird belong in the same class of clutch shooters as West.) Yet time and again his Lakers failed in the biggest of pressure situations. It was ironic: Mr. Clutch played for a choke team.

The constant losing ate at West. He was never one to shrug off a loss. He took it personally because each loss was a failure for him.

"He took a loss harder than any other player that I've ever known," said Chick Hearn, the Lakers broadcaster, in the *National Sports Daily*. "He would sit by himself and stare into space. A loss just ripped his guts out."

Tension Personified

West was as consistent off the court as he was on it. Every day of his playing career, he had the same routine, or perhaps it is better to say "symptoms."

On a game day, his nervousness would begin the moment he awoke. A long day lay ahead of him, but it was always a challenge to fill the hours.

As the day dragged on, West would become more and more tense. Throughout his career, he often took medication before games to calm his nervous stomach.

He would head over to the arena much earlier than necessary. Once there, the doctors and trainers would help him relax. This got more difficult as the years passed and the injuries mounted: a torn hamstring in 1962, a broken wrist and pulled groin in 1967, and muscle pulls and strains that would cause him to miss twenty-one games in the 1968–1969 season. And this list doesn't include the several times his nose was broken. It was another irony in his career; when healthy, he would routinely lead the Lakers in minutes, yet over his fourteen-year career, he ended up losing nearly three seasons to injuries.

"[A state of] unbelievable frustration," was exactly how he described the series of losses to the *Los Angeles Times* magazine.

Even when the game started, West couldn't relax. But as it progressed, the pressure decreased. And as the game wore on and each shot began to matter more and more, he found the pressure easier to deal with. Where others wilted in the spotlight of intense pressure, West bloomed.

"If I'm not nervous, if I don't have at least a little bit of the same self-doubt and anxious feelings I had when I started playing, then it will be time for me to quit," he told the

Orange County Register in 1990. "I must have that tension."

Injuries and Obstacles

And yet there were still the agonizing failures in the ultimate games. The Lakers returned to the Finals in the 1962–1963 season, despite losing West for more than twenty games to a torn hamstring. In the playoffs, however, he led yet another miraculous comeback, stealing the ball and firing a desperate shot from the foul line as time expired. But Boston closed them out again in six games.

The next season, a broken thumb in the second half severely limited West's ability to handle the ball and, as a result, St. Louis ousted the Lakers in the first round of the playoffs.

The team bounced back the following year after adding Darrell Imhoff in the center position. Once again they finished first in the Western Division. But then tragedy struck in the playoffs. During the first game, Elgin Baylor partially tore his kneecap. It was a season-ending and career-threatening injury, and one that seemed to doom the Lakers' performance. Instead, it proved to be one of West's finest hours. Playing six games in just eleven days, he scored 277 points—a 46.2 points per game average—and the Lakers triumphed four games to two. Although completely exhausted by his effort, he still had enough energy left to score 43 and 45 points against Boston in two games of the Finals. But the Lakers still fell in five games.

The next few years continued this pattern. The Lakers made the Finals in 1966 and again in 1968, both times losing yet again to the Celtics. They were eliminated in the first round in 1967, after having only the second losing season in West's professional career. The winner that year, however, wasn't Boston. Wilt Chamberlain, who had returned to the Philadelphia 76ers after briefly playing in San Francisco, had finally beaten the Celtics in the playoffs and then driven Philadelphia past the San Francisco Warriors in the Finals. This ended the Celtics' Finals winning streak at eight.

In the 1968–1969 season, the Lakers decided to acquire the only player who had beaten the Celtics: Wilt Chamberlain. This gave them a trio of arguably the best NBA players at their positions: the best forward in Baylor, who had made an amazing comeback and still played at a high level despite crippling pain in his knees; Chamberlain, the highest-scoring player in league history and an imposing defensive presence to boot; and West, the best pure shooting guard in the NBA, a man who had been denied two or three scoring titles only because Chamberlain was still playing.

Some observers worried that the Lakers would not be able to give each player enough chances to score. This proved not to be the case, and it probably underestimated West, who was often responsible for running the offense. Few players have ever been as dedicated to the idea of team play than the Lakers' guard, and the team ran like a well-oiled machine with Chamberlain's assistance.

Los Angeles Laker Wilt Chamberlain jockeys for position with Bill Russell of the Boston Celtics as he prepares to shoot during a 1969 NBA playoff game.

There wasn't any immediate payoff from acquiring the Stilt (as Chamberlain had been nicknamed), however. Once again the Lakers played Boston in the Finals, and once again they lost, dropping the decisive seventh game by two points, 108–106. They didn't know it at the time, but this would prove to be the last hurrah for the old Celtics, their eleventh and final championship in their remarkable thirteen-year run at the very top of the league.

The Lineup

When the Lakers once more made the Finals in the 1969–1970 season, they faced the New York Knicks. The series was destined to be one for the ages, a meeting of two legendary teams: the Lakers, with their wide-open scoring machine and soon-to-be Hall of Fame lineup, and the Knicks, with their own group of future Hall of Fame players (Willis Reed, Walt Frazier, Dave DeBusschere, and Bill Bradley), a group who were known as perhaps the greatest passing team in league history. In one of the many ironies of his career, West, who always put his team ahead of his own ambitions, played on a team known for its individual stars, and in all nine of his Finals appearances, he played teams that epitomized the concept of team play.

Two individual moments stand out in this great series. In the third game, after leading by 16 points at halftime, the Lakers trailed by 2 points with three seconds to go. West took the inbound pass and threw up a jump shot sixty feet away from the basket. It swished through to tie the game just as the buzzer sounded. Of all the clutch shots he hit in his long career, this was probably the most spectacular and best remembered. But as had happened so often, it ended up not being enough: the Knicks came back and won the game in overtime.

The other infamous moment came in Game 7 in New York. Willis Reed, the Knicks' all-star center (and league MVP) was injured in Game 5, although the Knicks were able to win the game without him. He did not play in Game 6, and the Lakers blew the Knicks out by 20 points. With the series returning to New York, it seemed as if the Lakers would finally be able to win their first title, although there were rumors that Reed would try to play. Even if he did, how could he hope to stop Chamberlain in his weakened state?

But when Reed limped out onto the court at the start of Game 7, it was all over. The Knicks,

Los Angeles Laker Gail Goodrich dribbles the basketball during an NBA game in 1970.

energized by their fans, won the game by 14 points, even though Reed could barely move.

It was another hard loss in a career of hard losses. And time was definitely running out. The injuries were having an effect on West, and his skills were finally beginning to fade, although his overall level of play remained high. He had been in the league for ten years and had taken a pounding. Seven times he had played in the NBA Finals, losing every time. It seemed that he and the Lakers would never break through, especially since they were aging rapidly as a team. How many years could the trio of Baylor, Chamberlain, and West remain on top?

When the Lakers could not even make the Finals in the 1970–1971 season, losing to Lew Alcindor (later known as Kareem Abdul-Jabbar) and the Milwaukee Bucks, the Lakers' long run as the NBA's second-best team seemed to be over. West went home disappointed and even considered retiring.

If he had been told before the 1971–1972 season that Baylor would be forced to retire after just nine games, his knees finally having given out, no doubt West would have predicted a dire season that would end badly. But instead, the 1971–1972 season was the Lakers' year, the season that they finally stood on top as champions.

The Lakers simply rolled over the rest of the league. They started out strong with six wins and only three losses and then ran off a thirty-three-game winning streak. No one seemed to be able to stop them. They had a good mix of young players as well as experienced veterans. They could play almost any type of game; their options were almost unlimited, whether they wanted to pound it inside to Chamberlain, or let the guards take over the game with deadly precision shooting.

A big reason for their success was Gail Goodrich, who teamed with West in the backcourt. Finally reaching the twilight of his career, West could no longer be the top offensive player every single night. He still finished sixth in the league in scoring, however, right behind Goodrich, who was fifth. Together, they averaged more than 50 points per game. More important, Goodrich's scoring allowed West to concentrate on running the team's offense, and he also led the league in assists.

The Lakers finished the season with a record of 69–13, the best in league history and a record that would stand until the 1995–1996 season. In the playoffs, they pushed past the defending champions, the Milwaukee Bucks, to reach the Finals for the eighth time.

Once again their opponents were the New York Knicks. The New York team had been rebuilt since the last time the two teams had met in the Finals, adding future Hall of Famers Earl Monroe and John Lucas; yet the team was banged up and missing their great center, Willis Reed, who had inspired the team to beat the Lakers in 1970. When the Knicks won the first game, played in Los Angeles, it seemed that once again the Lakers would fold under pressure.

But it didn't happen. Injuries cost the Knicks key players, and Wilt Chamberlain picked the Lakers up on his broad shoulders and carried them to four straight wins, earning MVP

Jerry West jockeys for position under the basket while teammate Wilt Chamberlain fires a scoop shot against the New York Knicks.

honors along the way. Jerry West was finally a champion. Typically, even in triumph he was not satisfied with how he had done. "I played terrible basketball in the Finals," he said recently, "and we won. And that didn't seem to be justice for me personally, because I had contributed so much in other years when we lost. Now, when we won, I was just another piece of the machinery. It was particularly frustrating because I was playing so poorly that the team overcame me."

The years of waiting and torment were at last over. West and the Lakers had finally won that elusive championship. Typically for West, when he finally broke through, it was with a team that will be forever remembered for its excellence. It was almost as if nothing would do for this incredible perfectionist, a man who could tolerate no weaknesses in his own performances.

Victory had come just in time. West knew that his career was fading. Now he had to begin to consider what to do during his retirement.

Architect of the Game

How much can winning one game mean to a player's career? West and the Lakers had finally won the big game. They had ended a city's frustration, had proven to the world that they were not a "choke team," and had set a standard for excellence that would last twenty-four years. But was it enough for West?

Perhaps nothing could be enough for this driven man. "I think I should make every shot," he said in his 1971 autobiography, *Mr. Clutch: The Jerry West Story*. Overall, he had an amazing attitude, considering that even the best shooter will miss nearly half his shots.

West, who was no longer as young as most basketball players, was constantly pounding on his body, making every game harder to get through. Although he had suffered many injuries throughout his career, he had gone out many other times and performed superbly with injuries that would have made an ordinary man—or even an ordinary player—remain at home in bed.

There were still a few frustrating finishes left in his career. The Lakers went back to the Finals in 1973, once more playing the Knicks, who had added another Hall of Fame guard, Earl "the Pearl" Monroe, to their lineup. The Knicks won once again in West's ninth and last Finals. He had lost eight of them.

A bad groin pull limited him to only 31 games in the 1973–1974 season, and the Lakers could not get out of the first round against the Milwaukee Bucks. In 1974, during the exhibition season, he announced his retirement. "I didn't want anyone to hit me again, I didn't want another needle stuck in me, and I was tired of losing. I woke up one day and said, I don't like this, and I don't like myself," he later recalled in *Mr. Clutch*.

"The average person wouldn't understand the pressure and the stress that I've felt in my life," he said later in an online interview with the Web site Dunk.net in 2000.

What does the ultimate competitor do when he can no longer compete? Once again, West entered a time of considerable adjustment, maybe the most difficult of his entire life. Once again he persevered and emerged at the top of his chosen profession, this time as a beloved basketball coach.

The first few years after retirement were extremely hard for West. His marriage to Jane dissolved, and the two quietly divorced. He was financially secure after a very lucrative playing career, but he had nothing to fill his time. He remembered the days when he looked forward to each and every game. Without his wife or basketball, his life suddenly seemed empty.

Lonely Days, New Prospects

For a while, he played a great deal of golf. Friends recall him being an excellent golfer who could have perhaps become a professional. West did seem to consider such a move. But the pressure of big-stakes golf was too great for him to finally attempt such a career. He was too much of a perfectionist to face the prospect of a bad round.

Friends recall West as being somewhat adrift. He moved from apartment to apartment. One of his friends, Gary Colson, the coach of Pepperdine University's basketball team, recalls West giving him many personal items: clothes, jewelry, even trophies and rings from his playing career.

One day Colson invited West to come to an event at Pepperdine. While there, he met a cheerleader named Karen Hua. To her surprise, West poured out his heart to her. She was moved by him, a very quiet man, so famous and yet so lonely. Soon they were spending a great deal of time together and were finally married in 1978. They later had two sons together.

Finally, in 1976, West decided to take on a new challenge: coaching the Lakers.

Coach West watches his team from the bench during a game in Los Angeles on January 28, 1977.

From the Outside In

In many ways, coaching seemed like an obvious choice. West still felt a strong need to be a part of the sport he loved. And what better way to channel his drive for winning than to coach a team?

His first season, 1976–1977, was his best. The Lakers had not made the playoffs for two seasons. West led them to the best record in the league. However, the Portland Trail Blazers later swept the Lakers in the conference Finals. Although the Lakers would make the playoffs in each of the next two seasons, they were unable to advance past the first round. West decided he had had enough. Constant tinkering by his boss, owner Jack Kent Cooke, irritated him. At the same time, West's perfectionism made it hard for him to deal with players with only average skills.

"I just felt a crazy desire to win every game," West told Ron Cook, a sports columnist for Post-Gazette.com Sports in 2000. "In professional sports, you can't do that."

"When it's time for me to walk away from something, I walk away from it" was how he explained his exodus to the *Los Angeles Business Journal.*

Even though he quit as the coach, West did not sever all ties to the Lakers. For the next three years, he served as a special consultant to the team, helping out in the front office and scouting talented college players.

It was not such an unusual move. Even during his playing days, West had demonstrated great insight in analyzing the strengths and weaknesses of his peers. This was all part of what made him such a great player.

In fact, he was unusually candid in his assessment of athletes. His takes on such players as Wilt Chamberlain and John Lucas, as revealed in his 1971 autobiography, were extremely accurate and estimated their strengths and weakness remarkably well.

Others recognized his talents, too, including the team's owner, who would bring West in to consult with him before the annual draft. (Later, when West became the general manager of the Lakers, he did the same thing with Magic Johnson.)

Moreover, in his fourteen years in the league, West had formulated his own ideas about building and maintaining a strong group. He was not pleased with the way the Lakers had been supervised during his long stay with the team. If given the chance, he would certainly try to create a great winning team that could achieve dynasty status.

Team Leader

West's chance to supervise the Lakers came in 1982, when he was appointed their general manager. Now he was the man in charge. Although he had relatively little experience in the front office, people familiar with his career and his driven personality should have expected him to excel in this job, as he had in so many others.

West inherited a team that was very strong. The Lakers had just won a title in the 1981–1982 season. They now had two of the best players in the league: Magic Johnson, already demonstrating a remarkable talent for pulling out games in clutch situations that reminded Lakers fans of West himself; and Kareem Abdul-Jabbar, one of the greatest players in the history of the game, and the man who would eventually set the all-time record for points scored. West's problem,

Jerry West, consultant to the Los Angeles Lakers, sits at an NBA pre-draft camp in Chicago on June 7, 2001.

then, wasn't to find a way to build a team into a winner, but to keep an existing winning team running strong.

In many ways, this was a more difficult job than starting from scratch. The NBA tries to help the weaker teams improve by giving them the higher draft picks; during his eighteen years as the Lakers' GM, only once did West pick in the top twelve.

The moves he made during his early years as the Lakers' GM were not spectacular, but they improved the team's ability to play well. He acquired players like Byron Scott, a sharp-shooting guard for the backcourt; A. C. Green, an unheralded power forward whose tenacity and big-time defensive play solidified the Lakers' frontcourt; and Mychal Thompson, who backed Abdul-Jabbar as the great center began to fade into the twilight of his career.

All of this insight into his players resulted in three championship titles by 1988. The 1986–1987 Lakers team is considered one of the greatest in the history of the game. As a nice touch, they beat the Boston Celtics in the Finals. This was the third time in the 1980s that a Lakers team had beaten the Celtics. To cap it off, the Lakers triumphed again the following year.

That season proved to be the last for Abdul-Jabbar, and although the Lakers would again make the Finals in 1991, they were unable to overcome the Chicago Bulls, who behind Michael Jordan would dominate the 1990s even more than the Lakers had the 1980s. The stunning loss of Magic Johnson, who had to retire after discovering that he had contracted HIV, the virus that causes AIDS, left the Lakers leaderless. The team finished under .500 the next two years and missed the playoffs for the first time in eighteen seasons.

This time West had to rebuild the team from scratch. He went to work, swinging deals that made them competitive again very quickly. In 1996, he acquired a key piece of the puzzle: free-agent center Shaquille O'Neal, probably the most talented center since Abdul-Jabbar. That same year he swung a key draft-day deal with the

Charlotte Hornets, picking up eighteen-year-old Kobe Bryant. Within two years, Bryant had blossomed into one of the highest-scoring guards in the league, a brilliant shooter who could score from any point on the floor. West finally added the last piece of the puzzle by hiring Coach Phil Jackson, the mastermind of the Chicago Bulls, who had helped that team win six titles during the 1990s. This move brought the Lakers their first championship in twelve years, a very nice send-off for West, who had spent nearly forty years of his life with the Lakers.

The End of a Legacy

After the 2000 season, West stepped down as the general manager of the Lakers, once more going out at the top of the game. The team he assembled looks to be a strong contender for many years to come, especially after their 2001 Finals victory against the 76ers.

At sixty-three years of age, West has seemingly achieved everything a man can in professional basketball; he has been an all-star,

Lakers general manager Jerry West presents center Shaquille O'Neal with a trophy for winning the NBA's MVP award in 2000.

Jerry West *(second row, second from left)* poses with a group of former NBA greats who were voted as the All-Time SuperTeam by members of XPRO, an association of retired professional basketball players, in 1996.

coached a team to the playoffs, and taken part in four titles as a general manager.

Is this finally all for West? Rumors persist that he may take another job somewhere, perhaps trying to succeed in the ultimate challenge: taking a team that has been a perennial loser to the ultimate prize.

It is hard to imagine someone as competitive as West ever stopping, even into his sixties. Yet after so many years of success, perhaps he can finally relax, at long last.

Maybe he can even watch a Lakers game. His nerves prevented him from watching most of them while he was their GM. He didn't watch any of their games during the 2000 playoffs either.

What mark did West leave on the NBA? Many great players have come and gone; some are barely remembered by fans today. West won only one championship during his run with the Lakers as a player, and Americans can sometimes be forgetful of the people who didn't win.

But the NBA knows how important West was for the organization, and it shows every time a game is played and on every piece of NBA merchandise sold. Look at the NBA logo: The silhouette of that lanky guard, dribbling the ball left-handed as he goes in for a score, is none other than Jerry West, Mr. Clutch himself.

glossary

assist   A pass from one player to another that leads directly to a basket.

backboard   The six-by-four-foot board that is fixed behind the basket rim, usually made of wood or Plexiglas.

backcourt   The players in the guard positions.

basket   The hoop through which the ball most go for a player to score.

center   The player most responsible for plays closest to the basket, including rebounding, scoring, and shot blocking; usually the tallest member on a team's starting unit.

court   The playing space for a basketball game, measuring ninety-four feet long; also called the floor.

dunk   A field goal made by slamming the ball through the basket.

field goal   A successful attempt at scoring by shooting the ball through the basket during regular play. Field goals are worth two points each, except when made from beyond the three-point line, in which case they are worth three.

forward   One of two players flanking the center, usually on offense. Forwards play close to the basket and must be good shooters and rebounders. They are usually taller than guards but shorter than centers.

foul   An illegal move or contact as witnessed by the referee.

fouling out   The ejection of a player after he or she has been assessed six fouls.

foul line   The line behind which a player stands to attempt a foul shot.

foul shot   An uncontested shot, worth one point, given to a player who has been fouled. The number of shots depends on the situation of the foul.

free throw   A foul shot.

front court   The players in the forward and center positions.

guard   One of two rear players on a team, usually shorter and quicker than the forwards and the center. Guards are responsible for advancing the ball up the court and shooting from long distance.

hardwood   The basketball court, so-called because of its wooden floors.

layup   A shot in which the ball is softly guided into the basket from close range.

MVP   Most Valuable Player, usually awarded at the All-Star Game and the NBA Finals.

NBA   National Basketball Association, founded in 1949. The NBA currently has twenty-nine teams in the United States and Canada.

pass   A move from one player to another, which may or may not include the ball making a single bounce on the court.

point guard   Guard whose main responsibility is to orchestrate a team's play and advance the ball up the court.

rebound   To retrieve the ball as it comes from the rim or backboard, taking possession of it for either team.

rookie   Player in his or her first professional season.

shooting guard   The guard whose main responsibility is to score from long distance; one of the team's primary scorers.

Naismith Memorial Basketball Hall of Fame
1150 West Columbus Avenue
Springfield, MA 01105
(413) 781-6500
(877) 4-HOOPLA (446-6752)
Web sites: http://www.hoophall.com
        http: www.basketballhalloffame.com

Web Sites

http://www.espn.com
http://www.nba.com/lakers
http://sportsillustrated.com/cnn.com/basketball

Jackson, Phil, and Charley Rosen. *More Than a Game*. New York: Seven Stories Press, 2001.

Lace, William W. *The Los Angeles Lakers Basketball Team* (Great Sports Teams Series). Springfield, NJ: Enslow Publishers, Inc., 1998.

Nichols, John, and Aaron Frisch. *The History of the Los Angeles Lakers* (Professional Basketball Today Series). Mankato, MN: Creative Education Publishers, 2001.

Potts, Steve. *Los Angeles Lakers* (Championship Teams Series). Mankato, MN: Smart Apple Media, 2001.

Spencer, Lyle M. *Meet the Los Angeles Lakers*
(NBA Series). New York: Scholastic
Trade, 2001.

Vancil, Mark. *NBA Basketball Basics.*
Sterling, IL: Sterling Publications, 1995.

West, Jerry. *Mr. Clutch: The Jerry West Story.*
New York: Grosset & Dunlap, 1971.

index

About the Author

Fred Ramen is a writer and computer programmer who lives in New York City. He is also the author of *Hermann Göring* and *Influenza* for the Rosen Publishing Group. A fan of the New York Knicks and the Syracuse Orangemen, he unfortunately had more than enough time to finish this book during the playoffs. Fred was a semifinalist in the 1997 *Jeopardy!* Tournament of Champions.

Photo Credits

Cover and pp. 21, 31, 52–53, 58–59, 62–63, 77, 80–81, 85, 91, 95, 100 © AP/Wide World; pp. 4, 27, 34, 42–43, 46, 68 © Bettmann/ Corbis; pp. 8, 25, 38 © Basketball Hall of Fame; p. 14 © Charleston Daily Mail/AP/Wide World; p. 98 © Reuters New Media, Inc./Corbis.

Series Design and Layout

Geri Giordano